Complete Hydroponic Gardening Book:

6 DIY garden set ups for growing vegetables, strawberries, lettuce, herbs and more

By: Kaye Dennan and

Jason Wright

ISBN-13: 978-1492794530

TABLE OF CONTENTS

K.Dennan and J.Wright

PUBLISHERS NOTES

Paperback Edition

Manufactured in the United States of America

INTRODUCTION

Hydroponic gardening has become more popular over the years for people who do not either have a garden or have a very small area in which they can grow their vegetables in soil. Apartment living and similar types of living styles mean that if a person wants to have at hand fresh grown vegetables on a regular basis they can do so by using the hydroponic garden system.

Hydroponics is the system whereby plants are grown in water not in soil. In saying that, the water does need to be infused with nutrients so that the plants do get the required food and if the plants are being grown inside, the use of correct lighting can be substituted for sunlight.

So what are some of the benefits of the hydroponic garden system:

- Less space is required for the return of crops
- Most systems require more monitoring than soil grown plants
- There is an initial outlay to set up (although not necessarily very expensive)
- The rate of plant growth, hence produce, is three times quicker than soil grown plants
- They can be grown at an easy to access level
- They are considered to be organic by many growers due to the lack of pests and diseases
- Due to the fact that plant nutrients are better controlled fruits and vegetables are not only bigger but also tastier

- The most used fruit and vegetables, such as lettuce, tomatoes, herbs and strawberries grow exceptionally well with hydroponics
- You can tend to them anytime during the day or night
- You grow all year round with no weather damage

Some disadvantages are:

- Because they need tending you cannot go away for a couple of weeks and leave them unattended
- You cannot get the nutrient mix right
- You cannot get your system to work properly

It is possible to grow a wide range of fruits, vegetables and flowers with excellent results.

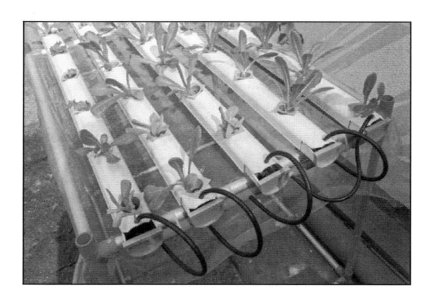

What is the attraction to growing with hydroponics?

Well, there are a few main reasons that seem to attract growers.

- The systems are ideal for courtyards and balconies.

- A plentiful supply can obtained from even a small system.

- Your garden can be at an accessible height.

- No need for chemical sprays

- Using them is quite a clean operation.

- If you live in a very cold climate you can still have fresh fruit and vegetables all year round.

If you are growing in courtyards and balconies you can have a small system sitting on the floor or you can run a vertical system up a wall and this really does mean that you are only taking up about 12 inches of floor space. A lot of older folk like the hydroponic system because they can set them up at waist height and tend to them without the bending over.

Because the plants grow so quickly, 3 times the normal rate, you only need to put in a few plants of each type that you want and then replace them later. Take a lettuce for example it gets to be full grown within 3-4 weeks rather than 10-12 weeks.

As there is no soil to worry about, there is no traipsing of mess into the house and no need for a long clean up afterwards. Tending to them during the growing period is quite clean and quick. You do not need to be worrying about composting and getting your soil 'just right'. All you need to do is find out what nutrients you need for the plants you are growing then keep adding those to the system as required.

Due to the fact that there is no soil from which a lot of diseases start hydroponic grown plants do not suffer in this way very much at all. Also if they are grown indoors you do not suffer the pest problem the same as growing in the garden. Even if you have a hydroponic set up in your courtyard you will find that the there is a lack of pests as well.

Ask anyone who lives in a very cold climate and they will tell you how they miss the fresh fruit and vegetables in the cold season. Well, with hydroponics you can have these available all year round. Of course, in this situation you will be growing inside and you will need to have it set up with lighting to keep the room warm and have the light that is needed for the growth of the plants.

Hydroponic gardening is often referred to as organic gardening. The reason for this is that the growers can use natural growth mediums made from natural compounds and elements. Home growers can therefore grow organically, but in essence when hydroponics is being used for commercial purposes it is rare that pesticides and other chemical products would not be used.

Another benefit of growing with these systems is that the water is recycled and therefore far less water is used than when a soil garden needs to be watered.

CHAPTER 1- THE COMPONENTS OF A HYDROPONIC SYSTEM

So what is needed to have a hydroponic garden system, and how does it work.

A soil garden needs the following components:

• soil

• sun

• water

• seeds

But a hydroponic garden needs:

• plants

• a sterile medium

• lighting

• nutrient solution

Before we discuss these vital components, however, let us first discuss the environment in which these plants are typically grown- indoor hydroponic grow rooms.

A Grow Room

Hydroponic plants are very often grown inside either in a kitchen area, in a spare room or in a garage. When they are set up inside for the growing of food for the family a small grow room would often be used, although not essential if the conditions are right without it.

The purpose of a grow room is to mimic ideal growing conditions of the plants that you will be growing. A grow room requires the control of lighting, temperature, humidity and ventilation. These grow room systems are available in the market, or can be a DIY project. Commercial growers prefer to have specific systems designed for their needs and to suit the type of plants they are producing. While the home grower will often also opt to design a system on their own, as it is cheaper and often they like the challenge.

When plants are grown inside in a grow room there is much less change of disease, pests and bird damage, as well as weather damage.

Plants that grow in grow rooms tend to be of a more consistent nature in color, size, shape and taste. This system also gives the best produce supply due to the ideal conditions.

Plants

Like any form of gardening plant knowledge is essential and hydroponic gardening is no different.

We cannot cover each and every plant here but if you are having any specific plant problem I would suggest you join up to a hydroponic forum (Google – "hydroponics" + forum) and get involved there. It will probably amaze you what people are actually growing in their homemade systems.

The use of seeds with this type of gardening is not very common because they do tend to float away. Of course you could start some seeds on a damp paper towel and use them when they have formed a few roots.

Initially it is probably better to start with small plants, cuttings or transplants. If you know a plant roots well then you can easily grow from a cutting. To use a cutting, just clean up the stem and leaves, take off the bigger leaves, dip the bottom in some root hormone and plant in your medium.

Did you know that if you take runners off your tomato plants that they will grow roots and form new plants?

If you are using plants that are in soil at the time of purchase, then rinse the roots off very carefully under cold running water.

Like any gardening you might just find that there are certain plants you can't grow and others that you have a huge success with. It will just be a matter of finding out why something is not working so that you get the results that you want.

Lighting

Lighting is essential when growing indoors because plants need light for photosynthesis. The choice of your lighting is very important so when you know what you are going to grow then get the right lighting to suit.

Sterile Growing Medium

A growing medium is what you put in your pot to hold your plant. Don't be confused in thinking that this has any purpose other than plant support, because it doesn't.

Because the roots are floating in water or hanging below the pot, the plant needs something to help it keep standing up and that is why the plants are planted in a sterile medium.

Any of the following are typical hydroponic growing mediums: sand, perlite, gravel, vermiculite, plastic and Styrofoam.

Nutrient Solutions

Mixing and using the correct nutrient solution is the most important part of hydroponic growing. It is through the infused water that plant gets all if its required nutrients. Without these nutrients the plants just will not grow.

Your plants will certain show if they are lacking in certain nutrients, just as they do in the garden. Such indications are yellow leaves, small leaves, small dry fruit, and so on.

It is because a hydroponic grower can immediately change the nutrients that their plants are getting that their crops can be so much better than soil grown plants where the nutrients need to be taken up by the soil then taken up by the plants. With soil problems there often needs to be a long testing process before a gardener even knows what to do whereas the hydroponic gardener should know before planting what his plants will need and then keep up that mix during the growing period.

CHAPTER 2- NUTRIENT SOLUTIONS AND TREATMENT

I mentioned earlier that plants have their own special needs as regards nutrients. It is folly to expect all plants to need the same mix of nutrients. In saying that most plants will survive quite well with a 'one treats all' attitude, but to get the best results more detailed information should be followed when purchasing your nutrients.

For example, if you were going to grow strawberries and cucumbers I would use two different containers. You would most likely want the best in your strawberries to be juicy, sweet and tasty, whereas you could grow your cucumbers with another vegetable and not notice the difference in a crop where the cucumber was maybe an inch smaller.

This of course, may mean having several set ups if you really want to take your hydroponic growing to the next level achieve healthier and better tasting crops.

Home growers can have several small set ups if they wish, which is not difficult to do but it also comes down to how many plants of one particular kind that you want to grow. Keep in mind though, that there are a number of plants that require the same or very similar mixes and therefore can be grown in the same set up.

More commonly two set ups are used when growing vegetables and flowers where the two mixes are quite different to each other.

Two smaller set ups are the **Drip system** as in the top picture below and the **Deep Water system** in the lower picture.

Deep Water System

Top Drip System

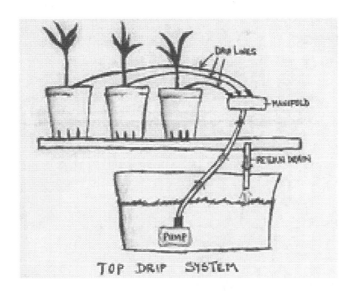

K.Dennan and J.Wright

The one drawback for a home gardener would probably be the cost of having to buy two pumps if you had two set ups.

Nutrients for Hydroponics

The major elements that plants get from the soil that need to be included in nutrient solutions in order for plant survival are carbon, sulfur, potassium, nitrogen, calcium, phosphorus, iron, magnesium, manganese, boron, molybdenum, copper, zinc, as well as the hydrogen and oxygen they get from water.

The list below shows how the plants use the various elements:

•   Sulphur: Sulphur improves the effectiveness of phosphorus and assists in the production of plant energy.

•   Calcium: Calcium is required for better root growth in plants. It also helps plants absorb potassium.

•   Iron: The Iron is essential to chlorophyll production.

•   Magnesium: Magnesium is a component of chlorophyll. Magnesium is involved in distributing phosphorus throughout the plant.

•   Boron: Its use is yet to be understood but it is known that it is needed in plant growth in very small amounts.

•   Zinc: Zinc is essential in the transference of energy in plants.

•   Molybdenum: Molybdenum assists the chemical reactions that take place in plant growth.

Complete Hydroponics Gardening Book

Interesting, isn't it, to see how one nutrient affects another and that is why it is important to use the right micro nutrient mix for each type of plant.

Hydroponic solution elements often come in the form of positively and negatively charged ions. They may also be grouped together in molecules such as nitrate, sulfate, and dihydrogen phosphate. There are various recipes available for making solutions of nutrients in hydroponics, but you can also buy them pre-made.

Making Your Own Nutrient Solution

Below are two growth solutions you can make yourself if you wish to, one for vegetables and the other for flowering plants. Organic gardeners have tested these recipes numerous times but you may want to try your own optional ingredients (you will see what I mean once you read this recipe). These are base recipes and you can experiment to get the best growth from your plants by adding or subtracting the elements.

Hydroponic Veggie Brew Solution, Per Gallon:

Miracle Grow Patio (contains trace elements) 1 teaspoon

Epsom salts 1/2 teaspoon

Urine (OPTIONAL - may create odors indoors.) 1/4 cup

Oxygen Plus Plant Food (OPTIONAL) 1 teaspoon

This mixture will insure your plants are getting all major and minor nutrients in solution, and will also treat your plants with potassium nitrate and with oxygen for good root growth.

K.Dennan and J.Wright

Hydroponic Home Brew For Flowering Plants, Per Gallon:

1-teaspoon high P plant food, such as 15-30-15, or 5-50-17, etc.

1/2-teaspoon Epsom salts

1 -teaspoon Oxygen Plus Plant Food (Optional)

1 -teaspoon Trace Element food (like standard houseplant food)

Home improvement centers do sell trace element solutions rich in iron for lawn deficiencies, and these can be adapted for use in hydroponic solutions. Prices for these larger quantity fertilizers are cheaper than the specialized hydroponic fertilizers sold in indoor gardening shops, and appear to work just fine.

Fish emulsion is another popular hydroponic garden additive, at least for greenhouses or outdoors, where smells are not an issue. Because of its strong odor, it is not recommended for use in indoor gardens.

Even if you buy rather than make your solutions, it is still important to understand how these solutions work.

As the plants absorb different nutrients from their solution at different rates, they will continually be changing the composition of that solution, and so you must take care to insure that the salt concentrations do not get too high or the nutrients too depleted. That is why testing of the water needs to be done. At first you may need to test each day, but you will soon know how frequently you need to re-balance the water solution and then you won't need to give it so much daily attention.

Nutrients for Different Stages of Development

Just as we need different amounts of food as we grow from babies to adulthood, so too do plants need more nutrients at different stages of their development. The fruit forming and growing stage of a plant requires extra levels of nutrients to cope with the growth. Changing the nutrient concentration in your solution as your plants enter into different growth stages will optimize plant development so that your harvest will yield larger and more nutritious produce.

Also, at different stages a higher level of certain nutrients is also recommended. For example, when your plants are just beginning to grow, your nutrient solution should be especially high in nitrogen, which is the nutrient that most greatly impacts early plant development. This means that a solution high in nitrogen will make your plants grow bigger faster.

When your plants begin to flower and fruit, you will need to change their solution so that it is more rich in potassium and phosphorous. This will insure that the fruit and vegetables will be the highest quality possible when you are ready to harvest them.

In order to have the best tasting produce, you should also flush your plants, as some of the nutrients that help your plants grow can also negatively affect their taste. A week before you harvest your crop you should stop giving your plants the nutrient solution and instead give them only water. You can also add a sugar supplement or a product like Clearex to remove any excess salt that has built up in your hydroponic system, but this is purely optional.

PH Balance

It is important that you test the PH balance of your growing solution. You can purchase paper test strips or liquid PH testing kits that will enable you to test the PH balance for your growing solution.

It is much easier to adjust the PH balance of your growing solution with a hydroponics garden than it is in your outdoor garden. This is because mixing, measuring, and testing can be done for the entire process completely in one bucket.

The solution's PH levels should remain between 5 and 6. Keeping these levels in check and providing the most nutritious liquid nutrient solution will ensure that your plant will be healthy and thrive. Phosphoric Acid is recommended for lowering PH and Potassium Hydroxide is recommended for raising PH levels. If you find that your tests reveal a need to adjust the PH balance levels, either to make them more alkaline or more acidic, you can easily purchase adjusters to complete the process from places online like Eco Enterprises or other hydroponic suppliers.

Water Quality "Hardness"

What is 'hard water'? It is water in which there is an over abundance of minerals - an excessive amount of calcium and magnesium in water results from ground water flowing over rocks under the ground.

It has been suggested by U.S. Consumers that 'hard water' is found in 85% of American homes but do not be concerned as the water can be adjusted to suit hydroponic growing. In fact, read on and you will see that it is easily manageable.

You may want to do a test to check the hardness of your water. A water hardness test will tell you the alkaline mineral ion count of your water. Total alkalinity test kits are fairly inexpensive and can easily be purchased online.

If your water tests over 150 parts per million, it means you have hard water.

The easiest way to work around hard water is to use a special nutrient formulated specifically for hard water. This nutrient will have been produced using the correct balance of nutrients, which will help to balance out the excessive alkaline mineral ions that are in your water. Using a hard water nutrient is the most convenient way of adjusting for hard water because you will not have to add a great quantity of chemicals to get your hydroponic garden to have the correct pH.

Oxygen in the Mix

Oxygen is as essential to root health in hydroponic gardens as it is to soil based gardens. Air or oxygen must be available for roots to develop and grow. In soil-based gardens, oxygen can be found in the many spaces left between soil particles, rocks, and gravel. This is why if water floods these small spaces or "pockets" for long periods of time, the plant will likely experience root rot due to the lack of oxygen available to the roots.

That often happens when people have pot plants. They think that the soil needs to be wet all the time and that means that the roots do not get oxygen then the roots rot and the plant dies.

If plant flooding deprives roots of much needed oxygen, how then is a plant to grow hydroponically where roots are constantly emerged in water?

When growing hydroponically this is taken care of by using pumps that add oxygen to the liquid solution or by exposing roots to air occasionally via a flooding and withdraw method.

Hydroponic bubblers are a common way to pump oxygen into the water and mix the nutrients in it. These bubblers add oxygen to the water so that plants will grow more quickly and have stronger roots. The bursting air bubbles at the surface of the solution also creates a spray to keep the grow medium moist and give the plants greater access to nutrients in the beginning stages of growth.

Ideal for the DIY hydroponic grower, another advantage of the bubbler system is that it is very easy for a novice to build and is perhaps one of the most efficient home hydroponic systems you can make. While other systems sometimes require a more in depth knowledge of hydroponics, the bubbler system is relatively user friendly and the materials to build it are inexpensive and easy to find. We will go over how to build a bubbler system later in this book.

Caution: Care should be taken when positioning your bubbler or air pump so that the intake draws "normal air". Advanced gardeners utilizing enriched CO_2 environments should note that drawing air from within these enriched CO_2 environments would serve only to kill the roots. The idea of the pump is to dissolve oxygen into the nutrient solution, and not to dissolve CO_2. CO_2, although great for leaves during photosynthesis, can kill root systems and in high quantities can kill humans as well.

Temperature

The temperature of your nutrient solution is also very important to the success of your hydroponic garden. The higher the temperature of your nutrient solution, the more difficult it is for the solution to hold oxygen. Not only does this carrying capacity for oxygen decrease, but also the need for oxygen in the plant increases with raised temperatures. This is because at higher temperatures, the rate of respiration in the roots is increased, and so more oxygen is required.

The optimal temperature for hydroponic plant solutions is 70-75º Fahrenheit during the day. For CO2 enriched environments, however, the optimal temperature range raises to 80-85º Fahrenheit.

Whether the plant environment is enriched with CO2 or not, you do not want the temperature to drop more than 10º or it will likely cause stress to the plants. You also do not want your solution to reach a temperature higher than 95º, or photosynthesis will begin to shut down. Keeping the temperature of your solution low will also keep pests in check as many of these pests reproduce faster when temperatures are higher.

Keeping some sort of control over these temperatures is why many hydroponic growers prefer to use the 'grow room' system.

CHAPTER 3- DIAGNOSING PROBLEMS AND SOLUTIONS

Since you are in full control of the nutrients that your plant receives, it is very easy to diagnose and quickly treat any problems due to lack of nutrients in your plants.

Listed below are some common symptoms of nutrient deficiencies and the associated nutrient that will help restore your plant to optimum health.

• If there is a decrease in the growth of your plant and leaves are yellow or light green in color instead of a vivid lush green, then you need to increase the Nitrogen in your plant's solution.

• If the lower leaves of your plant are yellowing and wilting, your plant most likely needs more magnesium.

• If new leaves and newly sprouted stems on the plant quickly wilt and decay, add more Calcium to your nutrient solution.

• Zinc is important to maintain the proper color of your plant. If you notice that the area between the veins on leaves is light, thin and papery or yellowing then you will need to adjust the amount of Zinc in your solution.

• An Iron deficiency will cause the opposite effect as a Zinc deficiency. If your solution is lacking the appropriate amount of Iron, you will notice that the veins of the leaf will remain a vivid green, while the remaining leaf area will be yellow.

• If plant growth seems to be stunted, and you notice that the plant has a blue/green color or a reddish tone, then you will need to increase the amount of Phosphorous.

• A Potassium deficiency can cause the leaves of your plant to have a thin papery look. The growth will be stunted and the leaves will have dead and decaying spots.

• If the leaf edges are curled, have turned blue or dark green, and all the new leaves on your plant are wilted, then you will need to adjust the amount of Copper in your liquid solution.

• If your plant has stunted growth and new leaves turn light green but the older ones remain a vivid green, then your solution is most likely lacking in Sulfur.

• A Manganese deficiency will result in a checkered pattern on lower leaves, consisting of both yellow and green. The overall growth of the plant will also be affected.

• If there is a deficiency of the mineral Boron, you will see a scorched appearance at the edges of newly sprouted leaves.

The Delivery Of Nutrients To Plants

If your plant is exhibiting micronutrient deficiencies but tests of your nutrient solution show this element to be at the proper concentration, the problem could be with how the micronutrients are being delivered. Some hydroponic systems may deliver the liquid solution to the plant in a manner that is too fast for the plants to thoroughly absorb. If this is the case, you may discover that there is a nutrient deficiency in the plant despite proper levels of nutrients in your solution. The easiest solution to this problem is simply to apply solution more often.

Now that we have discussed nutrient solutions, it is time to look at another crucial element of hydroponic gardening— lighting.

CHAPTER 4- THE IMPORTANCE OF LIGHTING

Lighting is one of the basic essentials of a hydroponic system. We have looked at other important growing elements such as oxygen, nutrients and water circulation.

Now we need to look at the importance of choosing the best light source.

When you are gardening outside in soil, the sun provides the lighting required for ultimate growth. Even with traditional outside gardening, however, different plants have different lighting needs. There are certain plants that favor direct and bright sunlight, for example, while other plants tend to thrive better in the shade.

When deciding on the type of lighting that you will need for your hydroponic system, you must first begin by determining what type of light the plant you are growing requires in its natural environment. If the plant you choose to grow requires full sun in a soil garden, then you will need to recreate the equivalent type of bright environment indoors with your hydroponic system.

It is also important to understand that all plants require periods where they are subjected to darkness. Do not make the mistake of thinking that the longer you leave your lights on, the better your plants will thrive. In fact, recent studies have shown that the amount of darkness a plant receives is as important as the amount of sunlight it receives.

Just as various plants differ in the amount of light they require, they also differ in the hours they like to spend in darkness. You will have to do a little research into what type of lighting the plants you are growing require, and perhaps experiment a bit with how long you leave the lights on.

If your plant has spindly growth, long spaces between leaves, slow growth, smaller new leaves, or fails to bloom (if it is a flowering plant), then it is likely your plant is not getting enough light. If this is the case, you should increase the amount of time the light is on and/or the intensity of the light it is receiving. If the leaves of your plant are scorched looking with brown patches, dying out and falling off, or look faded, it could be a sign that your plant is getting too much light and heat, drying out the leaves and therefore the plant should spend more time in darkness, and/or have a reduction in the intensity of the lighting it is receiving.

Types Of Lights

Lights used in hydroponic systems are known as grow lights. There are three main types of grow lights, and these are incandescent, fluorescent, and high intensity discharge lights.

Incandescent

Incandescent lights are the least expensive, but often gardeners feel that they are not meeting the needs of most plants. They are used mainly because they only cost about $5.00 and are readily available at any home and garden store. These lights provide about 150 watts.

Fluorescent

Fluorescent lighting is also relatively inexpensive and has been used successfully by gardeners for many years. Not only is it inexpensive but readily available in home and garden stores for about ten dollars. When using florescent lights as grow lights, it is recommended that you purchase the "cool white" type of florescent lighting. These lights emit less heat than high intensity discharge lights and are a great way to grow and clone plants.

One of the main disadvantages of fluorescent lighting is that you can only target it towards one area at a time. Manual rotation of the lamp is usually required to ensure that all areas of the garden receive adequate lighting.

When growing seedlings, however, rotating the light source isn't necessary, which is why fluorescent lighting is often used if you are sprouting seeds.

High Intensity Discharge

High intensity discharge, or HID, lamps are often marketed for outdoor use, but these lamps also work very well for the indoor gardener and can significantly enhance home hydroponic systems.

There are two varieties of HID lamps: metal halide lamps and high-pressure sodium lamps. Metal halide (MH) lamps create a natural looking light with a bluish tint. These lamps are popular choices for lighting in convention centers, stadiums, and gymnasiums. Many gardeners believe that metal halide lights promote vegetative growth and therefore a good lighting source for growing leafy vegetables.

High Pressure Sodium lamps emit a yellow/orange ray and are known for promoting flower growth. Depending upon the needs of your plant, you may even choose to use both metal halide and high-pressure sodium lamps together or interchange the two to promote both vegetation and flowering.

LED Lights

Now LED grow lights appear to be a more energy-efficient resource to replace the high-wattage HID lights. The light that is emitted by the LEDs has an extremely specific wavelength, which helps the plants to more easily absorb the light they need and mature faster.

The problem with HID lamps is that although they typically claim to emit 120 lumens/watt or more, there are considerable losses in luminous efficacy due to trapped light, protective covers and lenses, inefficient ballasts and unfavorable operating temperature. These factors often lower the system efficiency to less than 30 lumens/watt.

LEDs, on the other hand, have a luminous efficiency of 100 lumens/watt or higher, depending on the type and manufacturer of the LED used, but the focused output of the LED prevents losses from trapped light, and protective covers generally reduce output by less than 25%. Additional efficacy losses from higher-than-optimal operating temperatures and LED power drivers (which are generally more efficient than HID ballasts), the system efficiency usually remains above 50 lumens/watt.

The majority of hydroponic growing information you will find is based on the assumption that you will be using HID lights. Duration of growing cycles and therefore lighting cycles and nutrient levels may need to be altered slightly for LED light use if you are to get optimum results.

Complete Hydroponics Gardening Book

Research shows that plants need a number of light bands for the photosynthetic process. A number of manufacturers of LED grow lights offer 6 band, 11 band, and full spectrum LED lights for the optimum growth of plants. The red band is especially important for plants during the flowering season, and the blue band is required when the plants need vegetative growth.

You may need to experiment using different types of lights for different periods of plant growth. Gardeners will often try a number of different lights until they find one that best meets their plant's needs and their budget.

Understanding How Different Lights Are Rated

Color Temperature

One important aspect of lighting that you need to understand is a light's color temperature. Color temperature is measured in kelvins (K), and can be identified by the color of the light.

Whether a light is said to be cool or warm is based on the color of the light and not the actual heat temperature that the light emits. Light that is blue/white or very bright is called "cool" light, but it actually has a very high color temperature. Cool light measures roughly 3600K and higher. Natural sunlight is measured at 5500 K.

Warm light is either yellowish white or reddish white in color, and is about 3400 K or lower.

As a general rule, light that has a high color temperature is typically more expensive than lights with lower temperatures.

Color Rendering Index

The color rendering index (CRI) is a scale that measures the quality of light. The scale consists of measurements between 0-100, with sunlight and incandescent light both measuring 100. Plants show the most growth under a light that has a color rendering index of 100, however it has been shown that lamps with a high CRI often have low efficiency.

Lumens

Lumens are a measurement used to describe the intensity of the light. All lamps diminish in brightness over a period of time and it is important to replace them to ensure the health and vitality of your plants.

A garden requires between 1000-3000 lumens per square foot for optimum growth. Choosing a grow lamp should be based upon the amount of lumens the light provides and how much square footage you will need to cover.

Be sure to replace your grow light when it becomes dim, as dim bulbs will not provide your plant with an adequate amount of lumens. Never wait for the bulb to completely burn out, or you will jeopardize the health of your plant.

Elements Of Effective Lighting

Do make sure when purchasing your lighting system that the bulbs you buy fit the lighting system you purchase. Just as lights do in our house, the bulbs do need replacing so for this reason, it pays to purchase some spares are the time of purchasing your system. Bulbs need to be replaced quickly so that plant growth is not affected.

Choosing your lighting system is a vital part of maintaining and sustaining your hydroponic system. Manipulating the light source, ensuring that the correct amount of lumens are present for the area you are covering, and maintaining strong and visible bulbs that aren't dim will ensure that your plant will grow, thrive, and produce the bountiful crop that you hoped for.

CHAPTER 5- THE SIX MOST COMMON HOME HYDROPONIC SYSTEMS

Now that we know the most important elements of running a successful hydroponic system we can look at the smaller systems that are suitable for home cultivation.

Let us finally take a look at the various hydroponic systems themselves and how to choose the one that will be best for your plants.

There are six basic systems to choose from, all of which have their advantages and disadvantages:

- the water culture system

- the ebb and flow system

- the nutrient film technique system

- the drip system

- the wick system

- the aeroponic system

Water Culture

The water culture system is one of the most popular and basic hydroponic systems. There are several ways to do this.

A DIY system is to use a large box like container, something like a plastic storage bin and plants are planted into net pots which sit in holes cut into a Styrofoam board that literally floats over the micronutrient liquid solution. An air pump is included that provides oxygen and helps circulate air.

Or you can a system as shown below where the box has a lid and the holes are cut into the lid.

The water culture system is praised for its ability to grow lettuce quickly.

For this reason, it is the system of choice for many teachers who are instructing a class on the basics of hydroponics. The water culture system is advantageous in that it is quick and easy.

One major disadvantage of this system if using a clear plastic tank is that light reaching the nutrient solution can cause the growth of algae on the sides of the tank, but covering the tank with foil or dark paper will solve that problem.

Ebb and Flow

A very popular system is the Ebb and Flow System. Sometimes, this system is also referred to as the flood and drain system. In this system, the roots and a supportive medium such as rock wool are periodically flooded in a tray with a nutrient liquid solution. The liquid is then allowed to flow out into a reservoir chamber where it is stored until the next cycle of flooding. The system works with the assistance of a pump that repeats each cycle. The fact that the water is flooding the roots in the flow cycle and then not in the ebb cycle, means that the roots are being aerated during the ebb cycle so no bubbler is required.

One of the major advantages with the ebb and flow system is that it requires a minimal amount of water because the same liquid is constantly being recycled. Ideal for vertical systems as seen here.

The main disadvantage of this system is that it is dependent on electricity to keep the cycle functioning, and can therefore be difficult to maintain in the event of power outages, shortages, or malfunctions.

NFT

The nutrient film technique (NFT) system is another standard hydroponic system. In this system, the roots of the plants are suspended in channels while small amounts of an aerated nutrient rich solution flow continually over parts of these roots, keeping them moist but not water logged. This system can be tricky to set up correctly, as it is easy to either over or under flood the plants. Once set, however, it can prove to be one of the most cost effective hydroponic systems available. This is because this system allows you to grow many different plants easily over a period of time without completely reworking your system after every harvested crop. It is just a matter of replanting into the empty holes when older plants are removed.

Unlike other forms of hydroponics, which involve roots entangled in rock wool or gravel for support, the NFT system usually uses only a simple plastic basket or net pot to support plants, letting the plant roots dangle in the running solution. This means that when you are done growing a specific plant you can easily clean out your system and prepare it for another entirely new plant.

Like the ebb and flow system, the NFT system relies heavily upon the flow of the liquid nutrient solution through the use of an electric pump. If there are any power outages or shortages, the result for the plants could be devastating.

Drip System

Another type of hydroponic system is the drip system. In this system, plants are placed in a tray separate from the nutrient solution. A pump pushes the solution through small tubes that feed the plants from above.

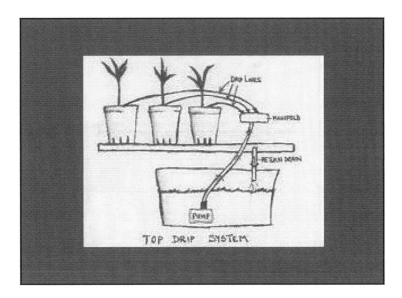

The number of tubes used depends on the number of plants being grown in the tray. Usually there is one small tube for every individual plant, and different ends can be placed on these tubes to make them drip either faster or slower, depending on the type of medium you are using and the needs of your plants. Mediums such as clay pellets that drain quickly and do not retain much media will need faster dripping tubes in order to provide your plants with enough nutrients.

The drip system may be either recovery or non-recovery. As the name implies, the recovery drip system uses the excess liquid nutrient solution in a recycling method. The overflow nutrient solution that runs off the grow tray is collected in the reservoir chamber, where it is circulated and brought back to the grow tray. This is both economical and highly effective.

One of the major advantages for using the recovery drip method is that the liquid solution is used repetitively. This proves to be cost effective. However, it does require a certain degree of diligence on your part to ensure that the PH balance and nutrient levels are maintained. The recovery drip system works with a timer and a pump that is submersed into the solution.

Another alternative is using a non-recovery drip system, you will not need to maintain the PH balance of the nutrient solution because you will continually add new formula. However, since you will not be using the runoff, you will need to manually add more solution as needed, and either make or buy new formula to add on a much more regular basis.

A major disadvantage to the drip system is that the small tubes that feed the plants clog frequently, so the gardener needs to be very diligent about checking that the system is working properly and that the plants are receiving the solution.

The drip system is also a very difficult system to build on your own. You are much more likely to have success with this type of system if you purchase one from a hydroponic system manufacturer rather than try to make one yourself, although even professionally made drip systems tend to clog.

Wick System

The Wick System is the simplest of all the hydroponic systems. A wick made out of an absorbent material like cotton rope is placed in the growing tray and extends below into the reservoir chamber. As the plant needs the nutrients from the liquid solution, it draws them from the wick.

This system is beneficial for growing a wide variety of plants and is a great system to choose when introducing children to hydroponics because of its simplicity. Large plants may tend to drink more of the solution than smaller plants, and unfortunately that can make it difficult for the wick to keep up with the plant's needs. This system should therefore not be used for very large and/or water-loving plants like lettuce.

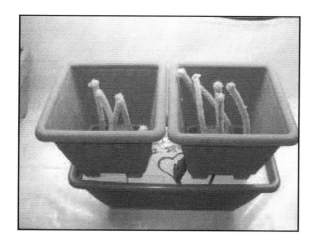

Personally I have not had great success with this system for vegetables but I do know others who are happy with it.

Aeroponics

The most advanced of all the major hydroponic systems is the aeroponic system. The aeroponic system uses a high-powered pump that mixes oxygen with the liquid nutrient solution and sprays the plant roots with a fine mist. As was the problem with the tubes in the drip system detailed above, the mister nozzle in the aeroponics system can become easily clogged and so cannot be used with anything other than the most high quality hydroponic fertilizers.

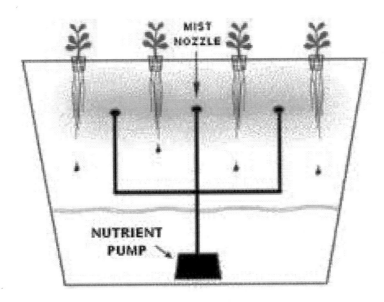

There is no real growth medium with this system, and so plants rely heavily on the continual spraying of the aeroponic mister to receive adequate nutrition. If the mister does become clogged, the plants will react negatively very quickly because they have no back up reservoir of nutrients saved up in a grow medium, and the roots can dry out quickly.

It is important that the aeroponic system utilizes a timer to ensure that the roots receive adequate amounts of the nutrient solution, and that the gardener checks that the mister is working properly on a frequent basis.

The continual misting of the aeroponic sprayer allows the plants in the system to grow at very rapid speeds, but the increased absorption rates of the plants cause PH imbalances and nutrient depletions to occur much more rapidly. This system is therefore very difficult to maintain, especially for the novice gardener.

Many aeroponic systems are complicated to operate and very difficult to build, but in recent years some inventive gardeners have come up with much simpler and easier to maintain homemade aeroponic systems. We will go over how to make one of these simple aeroponic systems, as well as several other types of homemade hydroponic systems, in the next chapter.

Considering the Options

Now that we have discussed the various systems, the first step to growing your own hydroponic produce is to choose the system that works best for your needs and the plant types that you would like to grow.

Your system or systems can be as small or as large as you need it to be. You can either purchase a system that is pre-assembled and contains all of the basic tools that you will need, or if you are feeling more ambitious, you can build one for yourself.

There are various plans quite readily available that will allow you to build your own hydroponic system. In the next chapter we have laid out instructions on how to make several of the simplest and effective home hydroponic systems for you to consider.

CHAPTER 6- BUILD YOUR OWN HYDROPONIC GARDEN

I have put together this basic guide to building a few relatively simple hydroponic systems. Although they may not be complicated to assemble, they are well-designed systems that will give you the basic foundations you will need to go on and produce bigger and more intricate rigs when you become more experienced.

These systems can be used for outdoor hydroponic gardens or they can be used for indoor gardening with the addition of appropriate lighting.

Germinating Seeds

For all of the systems shown in this chapter, you will have better success if you start with small plants from your local nursery rather than seeds. If you really want to start from seeds you can germinate seeds yourself in a medium of rock wool or vermiculite in a pan. Fill the pan area with 1/2 strength hydroponic nutrient fluid mixer. The 5-55-17 mixture of store bought plant food should stimulate root growth of the germinating seeds.

Use a very diluted solution in distilled water and keep temperatures between 72-80 degrees for most seed types (check seed package or nursery directions). Warm temperatures are very important, as many growers experience low germination rates if the temperatures are out of this optimal heat range.

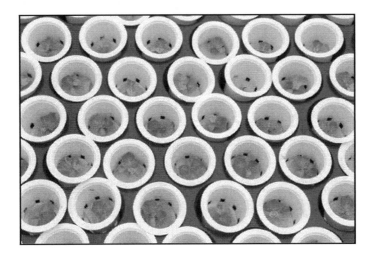

No light is necessary and may slow germination, so you may want to consider using a small heating pad rather than a lamp for warmth. Cover the germinating seeds with black paper to keep out light and place the seedlings in the light only once they have sprouted.

Deep Water Culture System

The picture shows a single pot Deep Water Culture system that has been bought and assembled. It shows the net type of pot that it is used in this type of set up. Of course there is the option of purchasing such a system or building one of your own. Below are the instructions to build one of your own which would hold more pots.

A DIY System

It is best to read all of the directions through once and make sure you understand them before starting your project. Refer back to them often while you are building.

What you will need:

- One rectangular fish tank

- Enough cardboard to cover the outside surface of the fish tank

- Enough contact paper to cover the fish tank sides twice

- A one-inch thick Styrofoam sheet

- Two or three plastic pots or colander type baskets. To gauge the space ratio, if the pots are placed upside down inside the fish tank they would cover less than half of the fish tank bottom. Three-inch plastic pots should work well for a standard sized tank.

- Enough gravel (or other medium) to fill the pots 3/4th the way full

- A fish tank air pump and hose with a rock air bubbler attached

- Clear Silicone caulk

- Hydroponic plant nutrients

- Water

- Small plants. Herbs like Greek oregano work well in this system.

- A bag of seashells

Tools list:

- Duct Tape

- Saws and Hole saws

- Scissors

- Magic marker

- Yard stick

- Spray bottle of glass cleaner

- Gorilla ® glue or any other similarly strong adhesive

Instructions:

(Steps 1-5 could just be black plastic if you are keeping this outside or in the garage.)

• Measure the fish tank dimensions from plastic lip at top to plastic lip at the bottom. This is the area we will be filling in with cardboard to block out light.

• Cut the cardboard panels the same size as the sides of the fish tank, with enough extra to form a cardboard box outside the tank.

• If you wish to cover the inside of the cardboard with contact paper. This will be the side facing the glass later and will be seen when looking through the glass from the inside of the fish tank.

• Tape the cardboard panels in place to form the box to slip over the fish tank.

• Run a strip of contact paper around the outside of the cardboard box. The goal here is to completely seal out light. This contact paper could be chosen to compliment the décor of the room.

• Set the air stone in the bottom of tank and then run the hose across the bottom of the tank to one of the back corners. Tape the hose down in place in this corner and then run the remaining part of the hose up the side and out of the fish tank. At the top of the tank tack the hose with bits of tape to get it to fit snuggly in the corner.

• Use silicone caulk to keep the hose in place.

Tips for Great Silicone:

Silicone forms a skin quickly as it dries and becomes hard to work with, and the more you mess with it the worse it gets. So have all of your tools ready before you start using the silicone caulking and then work quickly. When you are done, leave it alone until it is completely dry.

1. Before you begin with the silicone, place tape along the sides of hose about 1/4 inch away from original caulk line in fish tank.

2. Make a trowel by cutting a 3 inch square of cardboard and then snip enough off one corner so that when it is placed in the corner of the fish tank you can run it up the sides of tape without hitting the hose. This cardboard trowel will be used later to strike off extra calk.

3. Apply silicone generously over hose, in essence gluing and encasing the hose in silicone.

4. Use more silicone than is needed as the excess can easily be removed. When caulking it is best not to lift applicator away from the bead of caulk you are applying to avoid air bubbles from forming in the caulk.

5. When you are sure that you have enough caulk in the corner, quickly mist the caulk and surrounding area with glass cleaner. Then immediately start from bottom of tank with your cardboard trowel and move up to the top in one motion. This will strike off excess caulk and leave the hose encapsulated in a triangular shaped caulk prism running inside the fish tank's corner.

6. Once the silicone is dry pull off the tape.

7. Make the floating platform out of the 1-inch Styrofoam sheet. Now cut the Styrofoam sheet in a rectangle just slightly smaller than the inside dimensions of the fish tank. You can easily cut straight lines with a table saw. Test to see that the Styrofoam slips easily in and out of the tank but still fits quite snuggly.

8.   Arrange the flowerpots so that they are evenly spaced on the Styrofoam sheet and are no closer than two inches from the edges. Trace bottoms of the pots and cut out holes so pots fit snugly in up to the lip.

9.   If you wish decorate the top of the Styrofoam with light seashells glued down with Gorilla ® glue and let dry.

10.   Fill the tank half full with clear room temperature water and nutrient solution.

11.   Place the floating Styrofoam platform in the tank and ensure that it fits tightly while still having the ability to float up and down with changing water levels.

12.   Gently transplant plants into the pots in the Styrofoam, carefully arranging gravel around the bare roots without damaging them.

13.   Gently pour room temperature water through gravel around plants until the platform is floating near the top.

14.   Turn on the bubbler and enjoy watching your plants grow. Add water or nutrients as necessary.

Note: From time to time you will need to check the condition of the nutrient solution. You can do this easily by temporarily removing one of the pots or even the entire platform. This is also the same method you use to add extra water.

Building a NFT System

I have included here several different pictures to give you an idea of slight differences in parts that are used.

This is a basic beginner's set-up for an NFT system, but if you master this smaller hydroponic garden you will easily be able to modify the plans and make a much larger system simply by using larger pieces of PVC and a larger bucket to hold the nutrients.

Purchase plants from a local nursery or grow your own from seeds. Wait until your plants are about 4-6 inches tall to transfer them to the NFT system. When they are ready, remove them gently from the dirt or vermiculite, and wash them using clean water to get every last piece off of the roots. Then wrap the stems in polyester fluff and push into a small pieces of garden hose, or use the small cups as in pictures below.

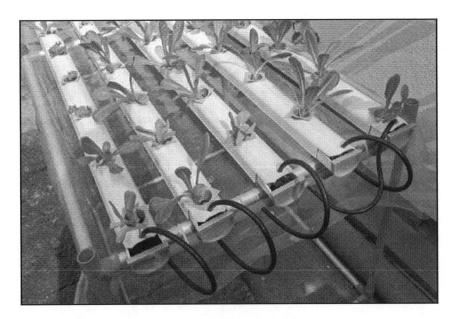

What you will need:

- One 5-10 gallon bucket

- Two pieces of PVC or ABS pipe, 8-10' long and 5" or greater diameter

- 16 small cups or pieces of hose for plants

- planting medium or polyester fluff is using the hose

- Four caps for PVC/APS pipe ends

- One water pump capable of pumping about 50 gallons per hour (you will obviously need a bigger pump if you choose to make this a larger system)

- Four feet of hose that will fit the water pump (often 3/8")

- One T-joint (or Y-splitter) that fits the water hose

- Four clamps for the water hose (one for pump to hose, and three for hose to TEE fitting)

- One air pump, air stone, and some airline from a fish tank

- One can of white epoxy based spray paint

- One can of black epoxy based spray paint

This picture shows a small pot that can be used in this type of setup.

Instructions:

•   This is an important step. Everything must be made "light tight." Paint all hoses, the bucket, the PVC/ABS, and the lid of the bucket with a layer of black paint. Let it dry overnight, then paint it with a layer of white paint so it becomes reflective and so help reduce the temperature of the nutrient solution in the bucket.

•   Take each of the PVC pieces and drill a 1" hole in the side, about one inch from the end. Then epoxy the caps onto the ends of the PVC.

•   Drill the inlet/outlet holes. These should be located on the caps of the PV.

The inlet hole should be as low (as close to the wall of the PVC) as possible, and the outlet hole should be as high as possible.

•	Cut two 5" holes in the sides of the bucket (close to the top), and epoxy the PVC in place so that about 2" of pipe, and the outlet hole, are inside the bucket and the 1" hole is facing straight up.

•	Place the air stone in the bottom of the bucket, and find a place near the bucket for the air pump.

•	Place the water pump in the bottom of the bucket (assuming it is a submersible one) and attach a hose to it that is long enough to reach the top of the bucket. Cut a hole in the lid of the bucket for this hose to go through.

•	Attach the TEE fitting to the hose, and then attach hoses to the free ends of the TEE. Run these hoses to the inlet holes on the end of the PVC pipes. Use clamps on the TEE fitting and on the pump itself, but use epoxy to attach the hoses to the PVC. This seal must be completely watertight. Let dry for 24 hours.

•	Put some water in the bucket and turn on the pump. What should happen is that the PVC pieces will fill with water, and then when they are full, they should begin to continuously drain out the outlet holes, and back into the bucket. If you are getting leaks anywhere, fix them immediately. If water is coming out of the 1" hole on the top of the pipe, then either your pump is too strong, or your outlet hole is too small.

•	Once you get it right, empty the system and replace the water with your hydroponic nutrient solution.

•	Place your plants into the system. The best way I have found to do this is to take a 1 1/8" garden hose and cut a 1" tube off one end then slit the tube down one side. Prepare the plant by wrapping the stem of your plant, just above the roots, with polyester fluff (available at most aquarium stores) prior to wrapping the garden hose around them. Then you can simply force the hose down into the hole at the top of the PVC arm. Another popular option is to use rubber stoppers or the small plastic pot as shown above.

- Turn on the air/water pumps, and let your garden grow.

The Ebb and Flow Bucket System

Ebb and flow systems are a very popular form of homemade hydroponics because they are rather simple and inexpensive to make. This system does require more attention and manual flooding of the plants than some other systems, but the amount of work required to make the system is minimal and it is easy to use, making it a great choice for beginning hydroponic gardeners.

The picture below is a vertical system and these systems work really well where there is little room and the ebb and flow system is excellent to operate with them.

What you will need to set up a basic system:

•   Two large buckets with lids

•   Several feet of rubber tubing

•   Gravel

•   A fine mesh plastic screen

•   Perlite, Rockwool, coconut fiber, or another type of grow medium of your choice

- Nutrient solution

Instructions:

- Drill a about a half-inch from the bottom of both of your buckets and connect them with tubing. You should have enough tubing to place one of the buckets on a platform while the other bucket, which will hold the nutrient solution, is left on the floor.

- Place a couple inches of gravel in the bucket that will hold your plants, then cover it with the fine mesh plastic screen. The screen should fit tightly to the sides of the bucket.

- On top of the screen, place the perlite, Rockwool, coconut fiber, or whatever other growth medium you have chosen to use.

- Place your plants in the growth medium in the first bucket, and then fill the second bucket with nutrient solution. Cover this second bucket with a lid to keep out foreign debris and dust.

- Lift the nutrient bucket so it is on the platform with your grow bucket. This will allow the nutrient solution to flood your plants.

- After your plants have been well soaked, place the nutrient bucket back on the floor. This process of flooding and draining your grow bucket will need to be repeated several times a day.

The Wick System

A third easy-to-make hydroponic system is the wick system. It is built much like the bucket ebb and flow system except that the two buckets are connected with a highly absorbent wick rather than tubing. As the growth medium gets dry, more solution is pulled up the wick by capillary action, eliminating the need to continually lift and lower the nutrient bucket.

The wick method allows plants to receive a steady flow of solution without being flooded and drained several times a day.

Simple Aeroponic System

Aeroponic systems are detailed and can be difficult to set up and maintain but that is not necessarily the case. This simple aeroponic system will provide you with quick plant growth that is characteristic of aeroponic systems while avoiding some of the common problems like clogged nozzles and complicated set ups.

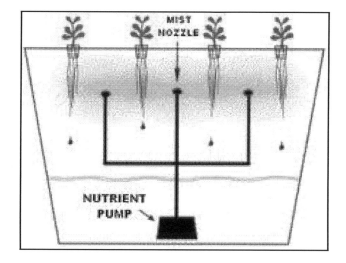

What you will need:

- A five-gallon bucket with a lid

- An old garden hose (or other tubing)

- An aquarium water pump

- A netted pot

- Perlite, expanded clay pellets, Rockwool, coconut fiber, or another type of grow medium of your choice

- Nutrient solution

Instructions:

- Fill the bucket with about a gallon of nutrient solution.

- Drill 1/16 inch holes into the hose every few inches. This is what will create the mist that will spray your plants with the nutrient solution.

- Attach the hose to the aquarium water pump and place the pump at the bottom of the bucket so that it is submerged in nutrient solution. A pump that can pump three hundred gallons per hour or more works best for this system.

- Coil the hose around the inside of the bucket. When you turn on your pump, you should have several small streams of water shooting out of the holes in the hose towards the center of the bucket where your plant will be placed.

• Put your plant and the expanded clay pellets, or whatever other medium you have decided to use, in the netted pot.

• Cut a hole in the lid of the bucket that is big enough to fit the netted pot in snuggly. You want the roots of your plant to be exposed to the spray from the hose. If they are not yet long enough, you may have to water the plant by hand until they grow to a sufficient length.

• Remember to make sure to check the PH and nutrient levels of your nutrient solution frequently, as the roots absorb nutrients very quickly when you are using this method of hydroponics.

Aeroponic Bubbler System

This is another aeroponic system that is relatively easy to put together, although it is slightly more complex than the garden hose and five-gallon bucket model.

What you will need:

• A large plastic container with a plastic lid

• Plastic cups

• An aquarium water pump

• An air stone

• Air tubing

- Perlite, Rockwool, coconut fiber, or another type of grow medium of your choice

- Nutrient solution

Instructions:

- Trace the bottoms of the plastic cups onto the lid of your container so that you end up with several circles on the lid that are the same dimensions as the bottom of your plastic cups.

- Cut out the holes you drew on the lid and suspend the plastic cups in them so that they fit snuggly without falling out. You will probably have to adjust the sizes of your holes if necessary to get a good fit. Do one first and get the size right and make the others the same.

• You can use solid plastic pots and make several small holes in the sides and bottoms of your plastic cups so that water can flow through them easily or use net pots.

• Put a hole in the side of the container near the bottom for the air tubing to go through.

• Set up the airstone in the bottom of the container and fill the container almost to the top with nutrient solution and water.

• Turn the air pump on. Make sure the water pump is working and there are sprays or water coming up and which will wet the plant roots.

• Place your plants in the plastic cups in such a way that the roots hang down and have access to the mist that your bubbler will create near the top of the container. Fill in the cups with whatever grow medium you have chosen to use. Place them in the lid and place the lid on the box.

• You should check to make sure that the air pump is working properly fairly frequently, and of course you will need to check the pH and nutrient levels of your feeding solution on a regular basis as well.

Chapter 7- Troubleshooting Your Growing Problems

It is difficult to give specific growing tips and instructions for hydroponics as there are so many variables such as water quality, system type, nutrient ingredients, and environmental factors that make hydroponic gardening somewhat unpredictable. What will work for one grower may not work for another.

We have managed to compile a list of troubleshooting tips that we hope will guide you through some of the common problems you may encounter with your crop. Keep in mind that these are just tips, not guaranteed solutions.

Many times a grower will have to experiment until he or she finds what works for their garden. Joining forums on the internet is a good way to find out what is working for others. Google: "hydroponic" + forums.

Blossom Drop

Sometimes a plant will drop blossoms simply because it does not have an adequate supply of energy. A problem with blossom drop will usually arise with its third set of blossoms, but in more extreme cases it can occur with its first set of blossoms.

Sometimes blossom drop can be corrected by adding phosphorus. You should also monitor the temperature levels between day and night conditions. If these temperatures are not satisfactory, your plant may suffer from blossom drop.

Blossom Set

Indoor growing can occasionally be problematic with blossoming vegetables. The temperature, light, and humidity of your growing room play a major role in the development of healthy vegetable blossoms. Make sure that your vegetables have the proper amount of light. Where possible take advantage of any natural light sources available to you, such as windows that get a lot of sun. Also keep in mind that most vegetables like cooler temperatures rather than warmer ones, so do not have lighting that will put your veggies under such intense heat that they get too warm. This is where the choice of lights is important.

The humidity of the room should also be monitored, as plants that dry out prior to pollination will have problems producing fruit.

Blossom End Rot On Tomatoes

There are several reasons why you could be seeing black spots on your tomatoes or why your tomatoes are getting blossom end rot. The main culprit is generally either a calcium deficiency or transpiration stress on the tomato's vine, or possibly both simultaneously.

One way you can identify which of these two problems your tomato plants are suffering from is to look at whether black spots are forming on the small tomatoes or only on the large ones. If your small fruit is affected, the problem is usually a calcium deficiency. Alternatively if the black spots are only showing up on your large fruit it is probably a sign that your plants lack moisture and are showing through blossom end rot.

Keep in mind that hydroponic plants will grow more quickly than plants that are in soil, which means that their root systems are often smaller. As plants grow they use a substance called calcium pectate as a kind of cement to bond adjacent cells together. Without calcium, the tissues in the plant become less stable and are likely to disintegrate, creating the dark spots you see on your tomatoes. The shortage of calcium and/or water stresses plants with small root systems because it is unable to take in enough water and nutrient solution to solve this deficiency.

Adding more calcium to the nutrient solution when you see black spots or blossom rot will probably not help, as the damage has already been done at that point. You could try adding a small amount of dolmitic lime, but there really is no good cure for this plant illness. The key is in trying to prevent it from ever occurring in the first place.

If you are experiencing hot weather, pour fresh water over your growing medium to ensure that the plant's roots are saturated. You want to make sure that your nutrient enriched water does not get too warm.

You should also increase air circulation around your plants.

If you do suspect that your tomato plants may have a calcium deficiency, use a foliar spray to counteract this deficiency before the plant begins to blossom.

Misshapen/Deformed Tomatoes

If you have tomatoes that have rough skin or are misshapen, it is usually a result of temperature factors. Colder temperatures can make your tomatoes tough and give them the appearance of peeled oranges. Too much variance between day and night time temperatures can also cause this condition.

Bolting of Lettuce

To put it simply, lettuce is a cool weather plant. Lettuce that gets too warm will usually bolt. Give your lettuce all the light you can in its early growing stages, and then keep it cool until it is time to pick.

Damping Off

Damping off, also known as root rot, is a fungus disease. It attacks seeds and causes them to mildew and fail to grow.

In hydroponic gardening, dampening off is usually the result of using your hydroponic watering system too much for the particular type of seed you are using.

Root rot can also occur if your planter is located in an area where it is too dark, cool, and damp. To fight off this condition you can apply an all-purpose fungicide and move your planter to a less humid location.

Droopy Leaves

If the leaves on your plants are droopy, make sure they are getting enough water. If you are using an automatic system, make sure all of it is working properly. If you are certain your plants are getting enough water, then the nutrient concentration may be too high for your plants. To correct this problem, flush the plants and only use plain water for seven days before starting your nutrients again. Leaves should be firm and hold their weight.

Insects

You will probably have to deal with aphids, white flies, or red spiders at some point during your gardening experience. To prevent these insects from taking up residence on your plants, keep your planting containers clean and throw away any dropped leaf matter. You should also try to keep your houseplants away from your fruit and vegetable plants. Separating plants is a great way to keep insects from spreading. If you act quickly you will find you will be able to keep control of these problems if they occur.

If bugs become a major problem for your plants, you can always use insecticides to get rid of them. If you use chemical insecticides if you wish as they are safe to use and will usually break down into harmless components within a few days. It is best though, to avoid spraying insecticide on the edible parts of your plants. Always check your insecticide's label for its specific warnings and directions, but as a general rule, don't harvest your fruit and vegetables earlier than a week after your plant has been treated with an insecticide, and you should always wash your crops well before eating.

If you are concerned about using chemicals on your plants, there are many organic insecticides that you can use. These are usually in powder form and are easy to apply. You may also want to alternate the insecticides you use so that the insects do not develop any immunity to the chemicals you are using.

Patchy Growth

If your plants have better growth in one area of the container than in another, it is an obvious sign that the nutrient solution you are using is not being evenly distributed throughout your system so check the rotation of the water and/ or pipes, etc.

Salt and Mineral Buildup

If you see white crystals forming on your growing medium, thoroughly flush the plants and the medium to get rid of the salt build up. Use only water on your plants for a few days before using a nutrient solution again.

Spindly Growth

If your plants are spindly and sparse, they are probably not receiving sufficient light.

Tip Burn

If the tips of your plants are starting to turn brown, it may be a sign that your plants are being overfed. Flush the medium and use only water for a few days before beginning again.

Chapter 8- Tips and Hints For Specific Plants

As we stated earlier in the book, almost all plants can be grown hydroponically, but below are some of the most common hydroponically grown food items and the conditions they grow best in.

Tomatoes

Tomatoes are the most popularly grown plant in home gardens. Everyone loves to grow tomatoes in their summer garden, but with hydroponic gardening you can enjoy the wonderful health benefits provided by tomatoes all year round.

Tomatoes are rated as one of the top food for us to eat in terms of health benefits. They are highly nutritious and are especially beneficial in reducing heart disease. They contain a wide range of vitamins and minerals. Tomatoes are also high in antioxidants and help ward off cancer, such as Lycopene.

When growing tomatoes hydroponically, you should keep in mind that without pollination, the tomato does not have seeds and it shrinks in size. Outside hydroponics might therefore be best for long-term tomato growers. Also know that tomatoes are very sensitive to temperature and prefer warmer growing conditions. Outside they require 6 – 8 hours of sunlight a day.

To pollinate indoor grown tomatoes it is really quite easy. Once the flowers start give your plants a little tweak with your hand each time you go near them. If you have them growing up vines or stakes just give them a gentle shake every couple of days. This is actually one of the ways commercial growers pollinate their tomatoes.

Lettuce

Lettuce is a favorite crop of hydroponic gardeners. Lettuce is a vegetable that is eaten frequently in salads and on sandwiches. Hydroponic gardening enables gardeners to grow all the lettuce they want in a relatively short amount of time. Lettuce also has many health benefits; such as it can help aid digestion and promotes a healthy liver. Lettuce also contains Vitamin E, Iron, Foliate, Potassium, Vitamin C, and Carotenes. Lettuce is very low in calories and comes in a number of varieties – all of which can be grown hydroponically.

Because lettuce loves water, it should be grown in a system that allows the roots constant access to the nutrient solution, such as the water culture system.

Cauliflower

Cauliflower is low in calories and makes it a great food choice and what is so good about growing it hydroponically is that it is a winter vegetable but by adjusting your settings it grows extremely well. It provides essential vitamins and minerals such as Vitamin C, Vitamin K, Foliate, Fiber, Vitamin B6, Trytophan, Manganese, Vitamin B5, and Potassium. Cauliflower has been linked to a decreased chance of heart disease and cancer. When Cauliflower is grown hydroponically, you can ensure that your vegetables will receive all of the nutrients needed to deliver a plant that is superb in minerals and vitamin content.

Unlike lettuce, cauliflower does not need very much water, and in fact over watering cauliflower can cause root rot. Because it is not a water-lover, cauliflower does best in a drip system. It also grows best if it gets around sixteen hours of light a day, so you may want to consider growing this plant indoors with artificial lighting.

Strawberries

At one point it was believed that strawberries could not be grown hydroponically because they do not grow well with wet feet. Nowadays, however, the hydroponic method of growing strawberries has become increasingly accepted worldwide, especially as the traditional method of cultivating strawberries was posing threat to the environment and the substance farmers were using to fumigate the soil for their strawberry crops, methyl bromide, was banned in 2005. The process of hydroponically growing strawberries not only gives greater crop yields, but is also environmentally friendly.

The process of growing strawberries hydroponically is quite simple and involves the following important steps:

• Cut runners from a mature plant to raise the saplings. Keep these cuttings in the Perlite to keep the root area humid.

- Wait for the roots to appear, and then dip the roots in a microbial mixture. Enclose the plant in a plastic cover and refrigerate it for at least four to five months.

- After simulating the winter conditions through refrigeration, keep the saplings in the hydroponic system in such a way that the roots sling into the solution. Do not forget to add the hydroponic nutrients to the system.

- Keep the PH level of the nutrient solution between 5.8 and 6.2.

- When the flower opens, brush it to spread the pollens to stamens and pistils.

- Harvest the plant when it ripens.

This process may be slightly involved, but it is worth it for fresh, nutritious fruits that are free of pesticides and pests.

Herbs

Nothing is more satisfying than cooking a meal with your own homegrown herbs and produce. Fresh herbs are generally rather expensive, and buying fresh ones every time you cook can mean a lot of trips to the store. Having your own herb garden at home not only cuts down on your shopping, it also insures you will always have healthy, tasty, freshly picked herbs available for all your dishes.

Different herbs have different vitamins and properties, but almost all do extremely well in hydroponic gardens. A hydroponic herb garden requires high temperatures and a lot of light, so it is best grown indoors where the temperatures can be controlled year-round. You should also pinch off the tops of your herbs if they begin to get too tall. Herbs will last longer if you keep them bushy rather than tall and scraggly.

The drip system works very well for herbs, and it allows you to have several different types of herbs in the same pot. Since each individual plant has its own dripper hose in the drip system, you can adjust the hoses to give more or less of the nutrient solution to each different type of herb in your hydroponic garden.

CHAPTER 9- CONCLUSION

Hydroponic gardening can be a very fun hobby, but more than that, it can provide you with healthy, nutrient-rich fresh vegetables all year round.

By now, you know the basics of what hydroponic gardening is, what its benefits are, and how you can make your own homemade hydroponic system. We hope that reading this book has taken some of the mystery out of hydroponic gardening for you and that it has inspired you to start a water-based garden of your own. There is nothing more satisfying than biting into a tomato or green bean that you grew yourself, and hydroponic gardening allows everyone access to that sense of satisfaction, even if they live in a small apartment with no soil to speak of.

Thank you for reading and enjoy!

About The Author

Jason Wright is a keen hydroponics gardener and has used many different systems over the years in his search to find what suits him best or alternatively the types of plants he is growing at any given time.

Jason is keen to share his knowledge so that other keen gardeners can experience and learn the benefits of growing fresh vegetables, fruit, herbs and flowers with a hydroponic system.

Don't forget to go visit the Amazon Author Page for **Kaye Dennan**, Chief Publisher at InfoEbooksOnline.com, where you will find more books on gardening, home based business and children's short stories:

http://www.amazon.com/-/e/B00AVQ6KKM

28210445R00045

Made in the USA
San Bernardino, CA
22 December 2015